leo season

"The launching of PREME MAGAZINE WAS developed through the REALIZATION that many creative individuals lack the recognition that they deserve. PREME MAGAZINE is created to give light to individuals from beginners to professionals to behind-the-scenes creatives. This includes photographers, singers, models, stylists, designers, songwriters, record producers, make-up artists, directors, musicians, and more. Our mission is to provide a platform and opportunity for individuals to showcase their work and talent."

4. SAMARIA

6. Earthgang

12. J.COLE

14. DRAM

34.

SMOKEPURPP

36. LIL B

50. CARLY ROSE

68.

XXXTentacion

72. NIGHT

SAMARIA

EARTH
BY ANTHON

J.COLE + BY ANTHONY SUPREME

15

IMAGES BY ALLEN jiang
STORY BY Gregory Gagliardi
Lucien Battiste - Gaffer/Lighting
Jay Mac - Assist

Gregory: Today I am joined by, and I am going be honest with you, I've always struggled with your name. Please don't take that offensively.

DRAM: Nah nah it is cool. You know the best way I put it, think of the word drama erase the a, and what do you get?

Gregory: DRAM, and how did you get it?

DRAM: Oh, it is an acronym. DRAM stands for does real ass music.

Gregory: We were talking off-camera about remaining true to yourself and how when I listen to your music; it is in touch — speaking of your music where have you been? We are almost coming up on a year of prototype we need something new.

DRAM: Bro, I am going to keep it a band the past couple of years like I really been going thru the ups and downs of life. I am dealing with many things, like regular things. I've built some bridges, and I've burned some. Family stuff, love life, keeping fresh it has been a roller coaster experience within its self. But,

Gregory: It is refreshing to hear somebody like you who has a huge smile, and every time I think of positivity and happiness I think of you say there are highs and lows of life, and I am feeling it.

DRAM: Oh yeah, I mean some days are better than others. On the ones that are not you got to make sure there will always be a tomorrow. So what do you do? You go to sleep and wake up.
I'm really excited for what's to come. This shit sounds so incredible, and I feel as though if I didn't go through the past couple years, I wouldn't be in the stance, to make it the way I feel as though it is.

Gregory: Is there anything you can tell us about the album or all that top secret?

DRAM: I'm still very much in the creation of the album. Definitely, have this record it's something like a phenomenon. Damn this is him, but it's not my typical main record, and as far as my real fans, they actually adore my singing more. So this time around it is mostly unadulterated singing. I feel as though I'm one of the best to do it. This next work will embody it.

Gregory: Do you consider a singer or rapper?

DRAM: I consider myself as cliche as it is an artist. But this time around I am honing in on this r&b, how about DRAM&B, my take on it.

Gregory: I remember listening to your last full-length album you had Young Thug, Erykah Badu, and Trippie Redd on there. You two made a song called Ill Nanna, which is amazing, what does that mean?

Gregory: So, how I would use that in a sentence?

DRAM: Ay, you left the club with Barbara? Oh yeah, yeah she got that ill nanna that shit snapping!

Gregory: I'm going to try to infiltrate Connecticut with this slang, see what happens.

DRAM: Yeah, but you know who birthed that? Foxy Brown, back in the 90s.

Gregory: Is Foxy Brown from Virginia?

DRAM: She is from Brooklyn!

Gregory: Who was from Virginia? Missy Elliot! You are from Virginia, right?

DRAM: Yeah, broodie seven five.

Gregory: Where in Virginia?

DRAM: I'm from Hampton.

Gregory: What is Hampton by?

DRAM: North of Virginia beach. It is the seven cities. On the peninsula side, which is my side you got Hampton and Newport news. Then you cross the water; the main ones are Norfolk,

Gregory: From me, I feel like Virginia does not come up in the hip-hop conversation as much as it should. We forget who is from there because that list is crazy!

DRAM: Okay yeah yeah, on a list, paper or whatever it might slip your mind. Regardless if you say it or not the people you are putting on the list nine times out of 10 had records made by these Virginia people.

Gregory: You guys changed music multiple times. Pharrell and Timbaland came out of there. They changed the shape of hip-hop. If there were one producer, we would never think you would work with who would it be?

DRAM: Oh, that's a good question! Toro Y Moi! He's the fucking truth!

Gregory: And he is hip-hop too, he got on Travis Scott's record back in the day.

DRAM: What I'm saying though, is we can do whatever together, glitchhouse, anything. His whole persona is the fact that he lives

Gregory: I would love to see that happen. What type of music do you listen too?

DRAM: It is a very wide range. When I was growing up, musically was my shit. The way my brain retains songs, you know those Timelife commercials where they had the collages of songs, big band, 80s rock ballads, and soul and body. There is this one song that I stumbled across its at the end of this Jeffery Dahmer movie its called "Lady Doubonette" by The Bizarros. It's so hard, its got that rock to it, and of course, all the way to (Young) Nudy.

Gregory: That's why I love to be around musicians and hear what they play. Now I feel like I know you better. Music is such a pure reflection of someone. If I were to go to the studio with, what would a session be like?

DRAM: If we are working together, it can be your greatest dream or worst nightmare.

29

Gregory: What do you mean?

DRAM: I am going to give 120% so if you are not coming to work, to catch these vibes then might as well not come at all. Because it is go time. It is fun, especially getting in with the right people and sounds.

Gregory: When you made the song Wifi with Badu was that made in the studio?

DRAM: No, so basically I went in dolo vibing around. Then I'm like okay let's get something going; I start hearing the bass. Then I started thinking and matter of fact I did need the wifi! So I went into the booth and freestyled it. That whole thing you hear was one take Queen Badu is my best friend in music, so I called her like Queen ima send you this record lemme get an opinion. She loved it. I wrote out her

Gregory: I've always been infatuated with Badu. I feel like if I spent 10 minutes in a room with her, my perception of life would change. That woman is magically, so many people have written songs about her. You mentioned Badu being your best music friend. Was there ever a moment when you got a co-sign from an older artist that made you take a step back?

DRAM: Yeah, damn anywhere from Q-Tip, Uncle Snoop the big homie, Queen Badu, and Beyonce the list goes on...

Gregory: Well, it should. You've made great music!

DRAM: Thank you!

Gregory: I'm a massive Frank Ocean fan, and he made a list of like 20-25 songs that inspired "Blonde" and your song $ with Donnie Trumpet was on there. Now I am not going to repeat the words because there is a word in there, I can't say.

DRAM: hahaha as long as you know

Gregory: But oh my god! I could be having the worst day, but if that song comes on, I become the happiest human alive.

DRAM: Even like to motivate. I was broke as fuck when I made that song that was recorded on a $100 mic.

Gregory: WHAT! See those are the things we as fans would never know. How many times you get asked "Broccoli" in interviews

DRAM: Shit! is my first interview in like a year and a half.

Gregory: Really?

DRAM: Swear to god.

Gregory: That's an awesome song, but there's a line that's struck me "at the restaurant with the why you gotta stare face" can you elaborate on that?

DRAM: It is like this. I'll make it even deeper; you know the flagship lounges in the club or at the airport that is the pure epitome of that. When I'm standing there tryna get me a burger or whatever everyone in there has that face like what are you doing here? It's like being financially stable, in here, living my life, how about you? It's classicism.

Gregory: We don't look the same, I don't have that struggle nor will I pretend I know whats it's like. But I do know whats it's like to have tattoos and painted nails and have everyone be like who is this dude? Why is he in this room? What do you do with those feelings?

DRAM: Tackle and fuel like Bobby Boucher in Waterboy. You take the good; you take the bad, you take them both, you take it all in. The thing

Gregory: Its authenticity, goes back to what we were talking about before. I
reviews is touring fun?

DRAM: Oh, tours are the greatest. The biggest thing I learned to do is perfo
coming up with it (a song), recording it, then performing it. The funniest th
are celebrating

Gregory: Do you make songs for live performances

DRAM: No, I make songs for the sake of making a song. So ultimately if its
performance. I feel like you start to fuck your shit up when you're like thi&
make it purely, like how life is. Somebody might think it is a facade, but no
live it for real. No matter how somebody perceives you, you still living you[
that.

Gregory: Absolutely, and that makes me think about your hit records. I dor
nowhere. Did you know how big "Broccoli," "Cha Cha," and Cash Machine

DRAM: Absolutely not. I am going, being honest with you, "Cha Cha" was r
the crowd hyped. I am back in Virginia at these local showcases. I had no i&

Gregory: From a fan's perspective, I remember going on a blog and seeing l
weed anthem, and it was like1 million, 2 million, 3 million, oh there is som
feeling like seeing a song explode? Is it like, oh my god?

DRAM: It's more like whoa, damn, that's what's up. But the thing is you n
defined by that. It's a blessing as well, the time that has been separated be

Gregory: Well, I'll be the first person to admit I loved the new EP, "DRAM

DRAM: Yeah, it's just some songs, nice transitional period. It's not like a s

Gregory: Yeah, totally. I remember seeing it on Reddit. You like to interact

DRAM: Yeah, it's cool they are really asking about a lot of shit.

Gregory: What else can you tell us about the new music?

DRAM: When this music drops, it will sound like whoa this guy has mature
he can sing his ass off. This is an experience; it is going to feel like I just w

about this, I've heard mixed

re many different parts,
to showcase it. It's like we

rd it will become a good
, and that is for this. Just
at, on the inside, you really
usic has to be as real as

say they came out of

sed to be something to get
goes down.

Lil Yachty hook up for a
g on here. What was that

song define you. I am not
ses you know?

's Name" it is an EP, right?

roject.

ne through some shit, and
some shit. You are going to

SMOKEPURPP
BY ANTHONY SUPREME

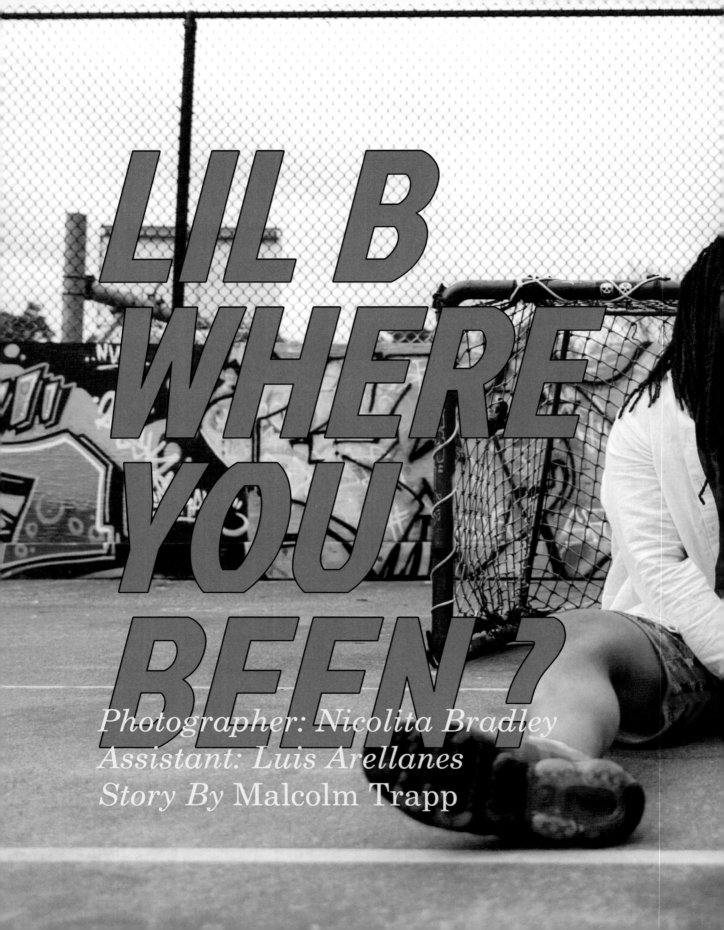

LIL B WHERE YOU BEEN?

Photographer: Nicolita Bradley
Assistant: Luis Arellanes
Story By Malcolm Trapp

California cultural influencer Lil B, known by many monikers, remains one of hip-hop's strangest phenomenons with over a decade in the game. Born Brandon McCartney, the self-proclaimed Based God has released dozens of mixtapes during his time, some of them including hundreds of tracks. The world considers Lil B an internet legend, and there's a reason why. "I'm in it to push the culture and push music, I'm not in it for anything," he humbly states.

Lil B emerged onto the scene as a part of high-school rap group The Pack with their breakout record "Vans." The sneaker anthem was released via MySpace and arrived at the peak of the Bay Area's hyphy movement. Nearly a year later, The Pack went on to drop their first studio album *Based Boys* under Too Short's Up All Nite Records imprint. "I didn't finish school because we were doing so much, so I was always struggling with traditional education." Unfortunately, after inking a deal with the short-lived label, they were dropped due a year later to lack of sales and eventually parted ways.

Following the group's dispersal, Lil B went on to kickstart his very successful solo career with 2009's *I'm Thraxx*. Since then, the Berkeley-native has unveiled nearly fifty projects containing several thousands of music. Some of his most notable works include the 2010 debut Blue Flame and collaborative efforts with Soulja Boy and Chance the Rapper. "Me and him did a very rare mixtape only released through SoundCloud and this is right before he won his Grammy," Lil B talks about his 2015 mixtape titled *Free*. Elsewhere, he exclusively shares information about their unreleased collaboration: "I have one more song with Chance the Rapper, it's about six minutes [long]."

In 2016, Lil B made an appearance in Frank Ocean's *Boys Don't Cry* magazine, which he initially teased a year ahead. The zine arrived fresh off of Frank's visual album *Endless* and came packaged alongside his critically-acclaimed full length, *Blond*. It featured acts such as Kanye West and Tom Sachs as well as two lengthy interviews with Lil B and Ocean's mother, Katonya Breaux. "I remember the last time we were talking, it was about potentially working on some records," B teases. "The relationship is love, it's always going to be love if I see Frank

Aside from Lil B's music career, he's given a number of speeches at college universities and became a published-author. "I feel like it's the biggest honor to be a part of any educational system because… It really did slow me down and make me cry. Even the American people bringing the thugs, the goons, in the house," B wittingly notes. *Takin' Over*, a book written and published solely by Brandon McCartney exhibits one of the most meaningful projects in his career. The print finds Lil B delving into subject matters of self-acceptance and fulfillment, while encouraging its readers to choose happiness over material objects.

Although considered a rap mogul by the masses, Lil B still looks up to many of hip-hop's rap veterans. Kanye West being one of them. "Without Kanye West there is no Lil B, there's no The Pack. No one has ever heard me say that," he states. Previously, Lil B released a song titled "New York Subway" that sampled "Living So Italian," an unreleased track that was slated to appear on Kanye and JAY-Z's joint album *Watch The Throne* a year later.

Humble of his beginnings, Lil B resides where it originally all started for him: the Bay Area. The 30-year-old artist is on a mission for motivational inspiration nowadays. In tune with his surroundings, B finds himself working on music and soaking in interactions from outsiders. Aside from touring and festivals, he details that he's lived in the Bay Area for the majority of his life in addition to learning how to produce records of his own. "It's been a really interesting journey, there were some times I had to take a break."

"I love the world, literally. If you're reading this, my fondness love to you," Lil B

carly

rose

photos by 70mm

styled by maz

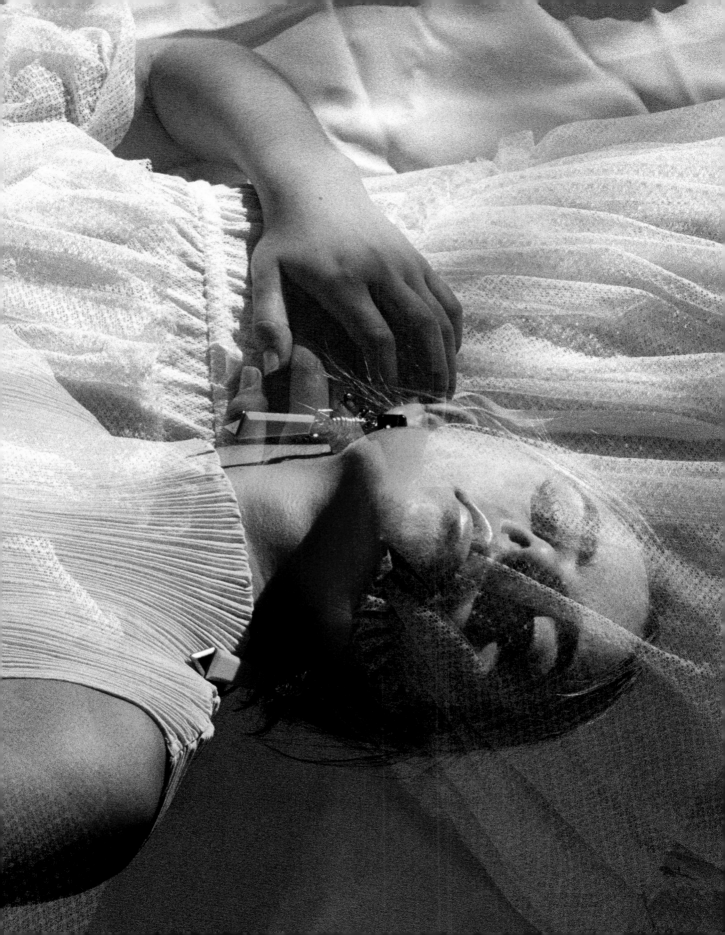

A singer/songwriter, with dreamy vocals, Carly Rose is cementing her name into indie-pop stardom. Her debut single, *Birds & Bees,* is a true testament to Rose's growth since almost 7 years ago where she garnered widespread attention from being the runner-up on the second season of X-factor, 2012.   Rose's path to her debut single has been unique and aspirational. On a friday in August, I sat down with Carly Rose to chat with her about her experience on X-factor, the fears she faced while taking a 7 year hiatus and what's to come next from the re-emerging star.

Walk me through growing up in New York and realizing that singing and acting is what you wanted to do?
It's not something that runs through my family at all. I was kind of the wild card in that career path. I grew up in the suburbs in Westchester, New York. My parents signed me up for a local class that was acting, singing, and dancing. Somewhere along the way someone told my parents that I should start taking it seriously. Plus I enjoyed it! ahah My parents were not at all stage parents.

 The class that I was taking had a day where you go to New York City to meet a manager, which was the biggest thing in the entire world for me. I read in front of them and they told me we see a lot of potential in you. You just have to get rid of your lisp. I was a child ahah. Then I thought oh great ok maybe this something that I could pursue. I then went to speech class I dont think I said this to anyone before. I eventually got rid of it and then I

I think theatre prepares you for everything , especially when comes to being a performer.

It's so true, it's so true. That's what I'm very adamant about. I'm always curious about how people do shows like X-factor with zero experience. I've never performed on live television before so I have to give myself some credit but theatre was definitely helpful in that sense.

How did you casted on X-factor?

X-factor sent out notices that they were doing virtual auditions. They set up kiosk in different places and the place that was near me for the audition was at the mall. So basically you went in and you had to have a certain amount of the song prepared. You had to pay to do it, it was definitely kind of sketchy. I didn't plan on hearing back from them but I was like, well, I will still try. I remember them only giving me a certain amount of time and they cut me off before singing my big note. At that time I was like no, that's the thing I need to do. I had to pay another 10 bucks to redo it. It just all seemed like a scam, honestly. We were there so I redid it. I end up hearing back from them like a few months later. And they were like, yeah come to Rhode Island tomorrow, you're an alternate and that's when you perform for the judges. There wasn't even a guarantee that I would get in front of the judges since I was an alternate. So I went with my parents and had to have a few songs prepared, we waited for hours and then eventually I sang

You've reached a high level of stardom at the age of 12, what does that feel like?

"Looking back at videos of myself with millions of views, I'm like who is that girl wearing jean shorts. It's just so strange. "

The only way I could describe it is that, looking back on it now it feels like a different person. I think everyone can relate to something like that rather you went through an experience like that or not. I look back and be like that's not me. Looking back at videos of myself with millions of views, I'm like who is that girl wearing jean shorts. It's just so strange. That was definitely an interesting jump into that world. That was right before social media became huge, like it is now. I didn't even realize the weight of what that would do for me. I gained so many followers and I didnt even know what that meant at the time. Now looking back I understand and it's crazy to see the reach that I had. It was interesting, I gained some great fans. Obviously it's been years since that and those that have stayed with me and have been awaiting this new music, those are incredible people that I appreciate to no end and intend to give them what they've been waiting for.

I could only imagine I feel as a preteen you're already going through a lot.

Right, all my friends little siblings and little cousins who are now the age I was at the time (X-factor) say, " I don't understand how you did that at this age, i'm just trying to figure out high school". Once you're in it it's just adrenaline and all that stuff that is pushing you through, you don't even understand what's happening.

Was there something you struggled with during that process?

"Staying true to myself and not molding to this character they wanted me to play."

X-factor it's a reality show and that was my least favorite part of the whole thing is having to have people tell you what to say and people asking you questions that get a certain reaction out of you. I at the time going into it didnt know to expect that kind of thing, especially a 13 year old. Having someone older tell you to say this or act like this in order to create this story arc was definitely something I struggled with. Staying

Would you do X-factor all over again?

"There's so many other ways to be heard now with Spotify and social media."

I don't think I've ever been asked that. At now, I don't really think at this age. Nowadays with the climate of everyone, I don't mean to it like it was decades ago but within the the landscape of music changed pretty drastically, with spotify other streaming many other ways to be heard now as a dician with go virtually unknown and you create music and following.

After X-factor, you decided to an almost year

"The music I was making wasn't what I wanted and out w

It was definite conce at the time. saying, " we for give you all world, you know whole turned ho was going to put me on the didn't different managers during this time begin and big names that I was very fortunate to rk with ss it became clear that what they wanted to do with me, did wha I really wanted. The music I was making wasn't really k tin out to figure out what I wanted. There were a few time it ultimately didn't feel right. And that was because they we pita ze or the moment and understandably so. I felt like it was more of a thi now and not so much of a creative figuring out the way music shou ade an artist should be developed. I also wanted to stay in school. I went ish highschool after that time and that was important to me to have th rienc to ground me. As a 13-year-old I wanted to have real life experience to w fro as a songwriter that was really important to me.

Were there any fears you faced?

"The fear would be what if all of this was for nothing."

I definitely noticed as I got older and started to understand exactly what it meant to have that many followers while on X-factor. As the years went on, the amount of people that engaged with me decreased. So once I started to get more of an understanding of the business, that was an unfortunate realization for me. Yeah, there were times where I was like maybe I shouldn't have waited, maybe if I would've done this right out of the gate this wouldn't be happening.

In those moments when I think that, I go back and listen to the music I was making at that time and listen to the music I'm making now, it's all worth it to me. At the end of the day, it sounds very cheesy but that 's all I care about is making music I feel good about and that I'm proud of, making the music I want to play for people, that is everything to me.

"The fear would be what if all of this was for nothing."

"The fear would be what if all of this was for nothing."

65

So you released your song *Birds and Bees* for your debut single, why now?

"It's a good taste of what to come without giving it all away."

Birds and Bees is a song that I did about a year and a half ago. I feel like it's a song that is a first good look into what I'm putting out. It's fun, and not trying to take itself too seriously. It's guitar driven, and more alternative leaning. It's a good taste of what to come without giving it all away. The rest of the music that I will be putting out definitely has elements of *Birds and Bees* but packaged differently. I wanted to start with stuff that would get as many people listening and engaged with me. From there go more towards less of what people would expect from me.

Birds and bees is a first good look at the world i'm going to be in.

How do you navigate the industry as an independent artist?

"I've seen both ends of the industry, and I wouldn't want to be in any other position."

I'm still figuring that out. I think it's definitely the time for independent artist and I think when I was signed to a label when I was younger that was the time. I've seen both ends of the industry, and I wouldn't want to be in any other position. If I was in the same deal I was in back then I don't think I would've had the freedom nor the time to devote to figuring out what my sound is and honing in on that I don't think I would have been able to do it.

I have great management team that helps me do the things that I don't think I could do on my own. I'm amazed at people who are doing it entirely on their own.

66

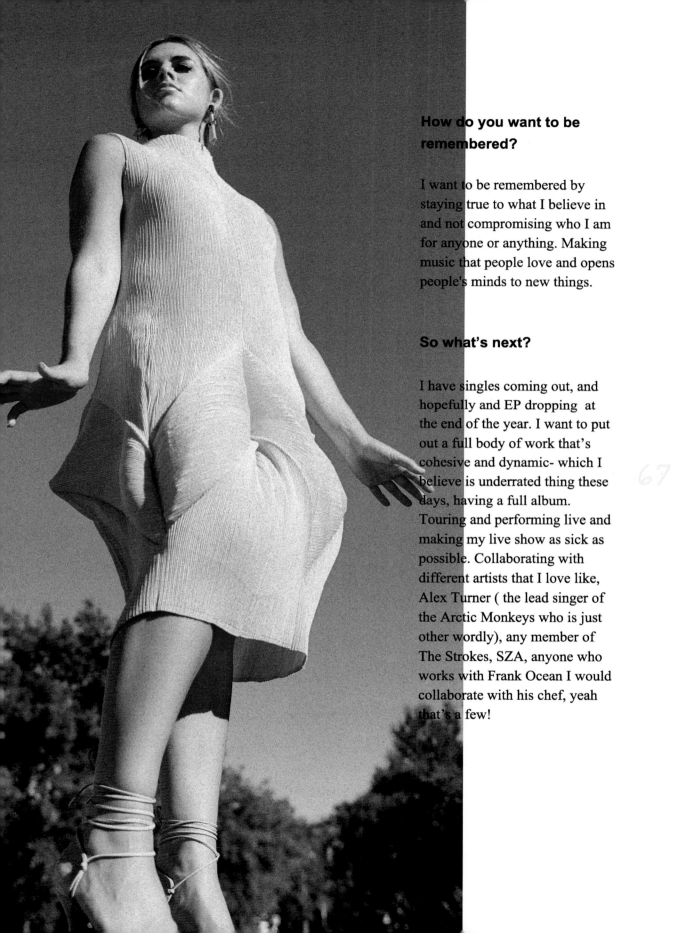

How do you want to be remembered?

I want to be remembered by staying true to what I believe in and not compromising who I am for anyone or anything. Making music that people love and opens people's minds to new things.

So what's next?

I have singles coming out, and hopefully and EP dropping at the end of the year. I want to put out a full body of work that's cohesive and dynamic- which I believe is underrated thing these days, having a full album. Touring and performing live and making my live show as sick as possible. Collaborating with different artists that I love like, Alex Turner (the lead singer of the Arctic Monkeys who is just other wordly), any member of The Strokes, SZA, anyone who works with Frank Ocean I would collaborate with his chef, yeah that's a few!

XXXTentacion

68

HT
ELL
HT
ELL

THE LAND
THE PEOPLE

Photographer Lamont Roberson
James Goldstone for Designer/Stylist

83

Talent: Topaz Jones
Photographer: David Katzinger
Hair: Quenton Barnette

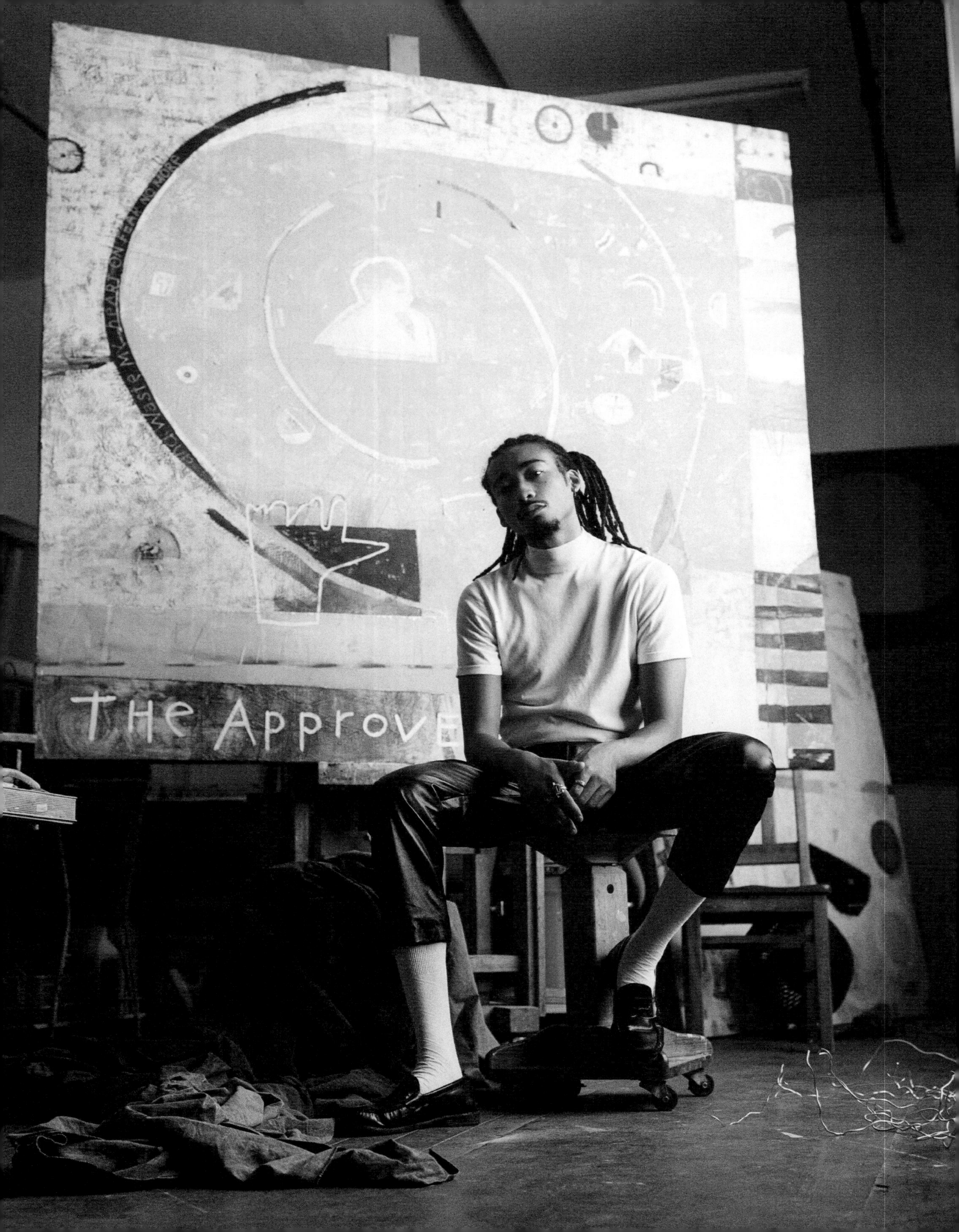
THE Approve

WHO IS TRAVIS MARSH

BY SHANE CARTER

1. For those who don't know who is Travis Marsh?

I'm a singer/songwriter ex-hopeless romantic and music addict.

2. Where are you from?

I'm from Ventura county it's about 45 min north of Hollywood. Most people don't know the area so I usually just tell people LA. Some real jazz heads may know Camarillo because it had a mental hospital back in the day where Charlie Parker was sent to get sober. He wrote a jazz standard about it called "Relaxin at Camarillo". Also we have the outlet malls, people come from all over for.

3. How did you get your start?

I've been playing music all of my life. First got a guitar at age 10 and shortly after started teaching myself a bunch of instruments. I got in to producing as an early teen and really have approached it as a career decision since then. By the time I was in high school I left and went into independent study to pursue music further.

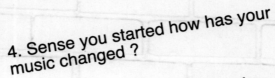

4. Sense you started how has your music changed ?

It has definitely evolved over the years. My love for guitar led me into rock oriented music as a young teen. I used to play a lot of music with my sister growing up, we sang together and I supplied her music. She really had a love for country and through that process I learned my love for different country instruments and started implementing those which led me down a more Americana and Country vibe. During this same time I kept producing and hang out with friends that were all involved into Hip Hop. From that I learned to appreciate the different rhythms and stuff of Urban and Pop music and started implementing those elements into my music as well.

5. You also do a lot of production works ?

Yes, as mentioned earlier I have always been producing as well. It has been an awesome journey being able to produce with different artists as it has exposed me to so many different talent sets and given me total freedom to work with all kinds of artists and through that process I have been able to learn more about myself and what I love and appreciate as well.

6. What are all the placements you've had up to this point ?

Some of the recent placements or

7. How did the come about ?

Most of them came about from me linking with the artist directly or through another producer. In some cases it came from me sending ideas to another producer that was working with the artist.

8. What did you learn from the producing side of things and how did it change your sound ?

Producing for other artists has given me the ability to further develop my ear. I've picked up on different things my clients enjoy about songs

and that has allowed me to experiment and reapply some of these concepts into my own music.

9. Plans for 2019 ?

I have a new song and music video being released on 9-19-19 called Give me a Reason. I've been in the studio the last couple months crafting a different sound than people are used to from me. I'm planning on releasing these songs, having some fun and continue producing other artists. It's the journey not the destination.

PREMI

ZAZA + THE UNDER
THE WEEKND

JUNE 2019

BA

Lightning Source UK Ltd.
Milton Keynes UK
UKRC010806101120
373112UK00008B/256